Fact Finders™

Land and Water

The Mississippi River

by Nathan Olson

Consultant:
Robert M. Hordon, Ph.D., P.H.
Department of Geography
Rutgers University
Piscataway, New Jersey

Capstone
press

Mankato, Minnesota

Fact Finders is published by Capstone Press
151 Good Counsel Drive, P.O. Box 669, Mankato, Minnesota 56002
http://www.capstonepress.com

Library of Congress Cataloging-in-Publication Data
Olson, Nathan.
    The Mississippi River / by Nathan Olson.
    p. cm.—(Fact finders. Land and water)
    Includes bibliographical references and index.
    Summary: Discusses the Mississippi River, its source, outlet, history, people, and
uses today.
    ISBN 0-7368-2483-9 (hardcover)
    1. Mississippi River—Juvenile literature. [1. Mississippi River.] I. Title. II. Series.
F351.O47 2004
917.7—dc22   2003012926

Editorial Credits
Erika L. Shores, editor; Linda Clavel, book designer and illustrator; Juliette Peters,
    series designer; Alta Schaffer, photo researcher; Eric Kudalis, product planning editor

Photo Credits
Bridgeman Art Library/New York Historical Society, New York, 18–19 (detail);
  Private Collection, 14, 16–17
Bruce Coleman Inc./C. C. Lockwood, 11
Charlie Palek/Tom Stack & Associates, 7
Corbis/Bettmann, 4–5; Nathan Benn, 23
Digital Vision/PictureQuest, 20–21
Houserstock/Jan Butchofsky-Houser, 26, 27
Hulton/Archive by Getty Images, 12–13
Index Stock Imagery/Ed Lallo, cover
Kay Shaw, 24–25
Kent & Donna Dannen, 10
North Wind Picture Archives, 5
Richard Hamilton Smith, 22
Tom Till, 1

Artistic Effects
Image Ideas Inc.

1 2 3 4 5 6 09 08 07 06 05 04

Table of Contents

Chapter 1

The Mississippi

As a boy, Samuel Clemens played along the Mississippi River near Hannibal, Missouri. His adventures took him into caves and to the edge of cliffs. He rushed down to the riverbank when a **steamboat** came to town. Samuel watched every move the boat and its crew made.

As a young man, Samuel worked on a steamboat. He also began to write. He wrote stories about life on the Mississippi. He signed his name as Mark Twain to his stories. On the river, boatmen shouted, "mark twain." This call meant the water was deep enough for boats to pass.

Samuel Clemens (above) wrote about life along the Mississippi River.

Samuel wrote many stories about the Mississippi River. The two most famous stories were about Tom Sawyer and Huckleberry Finn. These characters were based on Samuel's childhood friends.

The River

The Mississippi River flows about 2,350 miles (3,780 kilometers) from Minnesota to the Gulf of Mexico. It is the second longest river in the United States. The Missouri River, which flows into the Mississippi, is 190 miles (306 kilometers) longer. Although the Mississippi is not the longest U.S. river, it is the most important river for shipping. People call it the "Mighty Mississippi."

FACT!

The Mississippi River is home to about 240 kinds of fish and 50 different mammals. Moose and bald eagles live along the upper Mississippi. Alligators and muskrats make their homes in the lower Mississippi.

Some barges on the Mississippi River travel past St. Louis, Missouri. Barges move goods from cities on the river.

Chapter 2

The Mississippi's Path

Millions of years ago, large sheets of ice called **glaciers** covered parts of North America. Later, when the glaciers melted, lakes and rivers formed. The Mississippi River was one of the longest rivers formed by the glaciers.

The Upper Mississippi

The upper Mississippi begins as a small stream. It flows out of Lake Itasca in northern Minnesota. It twists and turns through lakes and over waterfalls.

N
W · E
S

Lake
Itasca

MINNESOTA

Missouri River

WISCONSIN

St. Paul
Minneapolis

Mississippi River

IOWA

UNITED STATES

Illinois River

ILLINOIS

Missouri River

St. Louis

Ohio River

MISSOURI

KENTUCKY

TENNESSEE

ARKANSAS

Tennessee River

Arkansas River

Memphis

MISSISSIPPI

LOUISIANA

Mississippi River

New Orleans

R
O
C
K
Y

M
O
U
N
T
A
I
N
S

LEGEND
• City
Mountains
River

0 ——— 250 Miles
0 ——— 250 KM

Gulf of Mexico

9

Steep cliffs and bluffs line the upper Mississippi. The river is narrow and the water moves fast. **Locks** and **dams** along the upper Mississippi let boats travel from Minnesota to Missouri. The upper Mississippi ends near St. Louis, Missouri.

The Middle Mississippi

In the middle section, two great rivers join the Mississippi. The Missouri River flows from the west. The Ohio River comes from the east. These rivers add large amounts of water and **sediment** to the Mississippi.

Bluffs line the shores of the upper Mississippi River.

A raindrop that falls in Lake Itasca would travel to the Gulf of Mexico in about 90 days.

The Lower Mississippi

The Mississippi changes again in the lower section. As the river flows south, it moves more sediment. The sediment settles as the Mississippi reaches southern Louisiana. Piles of sediment affect the river's flow. The sediment breaks the river into many small streams. This area is called the **delta**. The Mississippi ends as the delta meets the Gulf of Mexico.

At the Mississippi delta, the river breaks into
▼ small streams.

Chapter 3

The Mississippi's People

Around A.D. 800, native people began to live along the Mississippi. They built large mounds out of dirt. They used the mounds as forts and places to worship. Nobody is sure why, but the Mound Builders disappeared in the 1500s. Today, some of their mounds remain along the banks of the Mississippi.

By the 1500s, other American Indians lived near the river. The Sioux and Algonquian tribes settled along the upper Mississippi. Other Indian tribes lived farther down the river. The Indians used the river for its water and fish. They traveled in canoes and on rafts.

American Indians lived along the Mississippi. They traveled in canoes on the river.

Exploration

In 1541, life along the Mississippi changed. Explorers came from Europe. Hernando de Soto of Spain was the first European to see the river. He came to look for gold and claimed the river for Spain.

▲ Hernando de Soto (center) was the first European to see the Mississippi River.

Jolliet and Marquette

In 1673, Frenchmen Louis Jolliet and Father Jacques Marquette explored the Mississippi. They became friends with the American Indians they met. The Indians helped guide them down the river. Along the way, Jolliet made the first maps of the Mississippi.

Claiming the Land

In 1682, French explorer René-Robert Cavelier traveled down the river to the Gulf of Mexico. Cavelier was known as Sieur de La Salle. He claimed the land from the Mississippi River to the Rocky Mountains for France.

Chapter 4

Trade and Growth

In 1803, U.S. President Thomas Jefferson made the Louisiana Purchase. He bought the land between the Mississippi River and the Rocky Mountains from France. The Mississippi River was an important part of this purchase.

Traveling on the River

Americans were eager to use the Mississippi River. They began to ship goods on the river. Traveling down the river meant that people could trade goods faster and easier than by land. But traveling up the river was hard work. Many boats could not handle the Mississippi's strong flow.

This engraving by J. Wells shows boats traveling on the Mississippi River near New Orleans, Louisiana, in 1830.

The Steamboat

In 1807, Robert Fulton changed river travel. He built a steamboat with a large **paddle wheel** on the back. An engine used steam to move the wheel and push the boat through the water.

Fulton's steamboat was faster and safer than smaller boats. Soon, many steamboats traveled easily up and down the Mississippi River. They carried people and supplies.

Cities Grow

The cities where steamboats stopped along the Mississippi grew. Many people came to St. Louis, Missouri, because of river trade. Steamboats traveling on both the Mississippi and Missouri Rivers stopped in St. Louis.

Steamboats brought people and goods to cities. St. Louis, Missouri, grew because of its location near the river.

The cities of Memphis, Tennessee, and New Orleans, Louisiana, also grew because of river trade. Cotton grown on farms along the Mississippi was brought to Memphis. Steamboats then shipped the cotton down to the port city of New Orleans. There, cotton was loaded onto ships sailing to Europe.

FACT!

President Thomas Jefferson paid less than three cents an acre for the land he bought in the Louisiana Purchase. The area of land he bought from France covered 828,000 square miles (2,144,520 square kilometers).

Chapter 5

Industry

In the 1900s, **barges** began to carry goods up and down the Mississippi. These long, flat boats can be tied together to make a **bargetow**. Powerful **tugboats** push bargetows up and down the river. Bargetows can carry more **cargo** and travel the river much faster than steamboats. A bargetow with 14 barges can carry as much cargo as 140 steamboats.

People built factories along the Mississippi. Some factories made steel and paper. Other factories produced electricity. These factories used the Mississippi to ship their products.

Tugboats push barges up the Mississippi River.

Factories also used the river water to cool their machines. Working machines would get hot. People pumped river water though the machines' engines. This process kept the engines from becoming too hot.

The Champion International Paper Company is located on the Mississippi River in Sartell, Minnesota.

Environmental Effects

Bargetows and factories helped business. But industry has harmed the Mississippi's **environment**. Bargetows move large amounts of sediment. This rock and dirt turn the water muddy. Sediment can harm the places where fish and animals live.

Some factories dumped chemical waste into the Mississippi. This waste polluted the water. The dirty water killed animals living in and along the river. Today, it is against the law for companies to dump waste into the river.

Harmful chemicals once entered ▼ the river from open drain pipes.

Chapter 6

The Mississippi Today

Businesses continue to use the Mississippi. Bargetows carry wheat, corn, and other crops from the upper Mississippi to the South.

In the delta, fishing is a big business. Fishing companies catch fish, such as carp and catfish, in the river. They also net animals like crabs and shrimp from the river delta.

Oil and gas companies operate near the delta. They search along the river and in the Gulf of Mexico for new fuel sources.

Visitors to Lake Itasca State Park in Minnesota can walk across the Mississippi River.

Tourism

Tourism is important along the river. Tourists visit the many parks near the river. They can learn the history of the steamboat on a steamboat cruise.

Tourists also visit cities along the river. People travel to Minneapolis and St. Paul, Minnesota, to visit museums and historical sites near the river. There, people can learn about the history of the river and its early people and industry. St. Louis and New Orleans are also popular tourist spots on the river.

Tourists can travel up the Mississippi on paddle wheel steamboats.

▲ Skyscrapers
line the shores
of the river at
New Orleans,
Louisiana.

For thousands of years, people have used the Mississippi River. American Indians used the river for food and water. Explorers used the river to find new land. Americans used the river to ship goods. Today, the Mississippi remains an important river for the United States. People will continue to think of new ways to use the Mighty Mississippi.

Glossary

barge (BARJ)—a long, flat boat used to move cargo

bargetow (BARJ-toh)—a group of barges tied together and pushed by a tugboat

cargo (KAR-goh)—goods that are carried from one place to another

dam (DAM)—a strong wall built across a stream or river to hold water back

delta (DEL-tuh)—an area of land where a river enters the sea or ocean

environment (en-VYE-ruhn-muhnt)—the natural world of the land, water, and air

glacier (GLAY-shur)—a large mass of slowly moving ice

lock (LOK)—an area of water with gates at both ends; locks help barges move from one water level to another.

paddle wheel (PAD-uhl WHEEL)—a large wheel with paddles arranged around it; paddle wheels move some boats through water.

sediment (SED-uh-muhnt)—bits of rock and sand mixed with mud and carried by water

steamboat (STEEM-boht)—a boat powered by a steam engine

tugboat (TUHG-boht)—a small powerful boat that pulls or pushes ships and barges

Internet Sites

FactHound offers a safe, fun way to find Internet sites related to this book. All of the sites on FactHound have been researched by our staff.

Here's how:

1. Visit *www.facthound.com*
2. Type in this special code **0736824839** for age-appropriate sites. Or enter a search word related to this book for a more general search.
3. Click on the **Fetch It** button.

FactHound will fetch the best sites for you!

Read More

Adil, Janeen R. *The Mississippi River.* Natural Wonders. Mankato, Minn.: Weigl Publishers, 2003.

Lourie, Peter. *Mississippi River: A Journey Down the Father of Waters.* Honesdale, Penn.: Boyds Mills Press, 2000.

Prevost, John F. *Mississippi River.* Rivers and Lakes. Edina, Minn.: Abdo, 2002.

Walsh, Kieran. *The Mississippi.* Great Rivers of the World. Milwaukee: World Almanac, 2003.

Index